THE OFFICIAL
Arsenal
ANNUAL 2014

Written by Chas Newkey-Burden
(with additional research by Rob Kemp)

Designed by Brian Thomson

A Grange Publication

£7.99

Contents

Dear Supporter,

Welcome to the Official Arsenal Annual 2014.

The 2012/13 season was a challenging one for Arsenal yet we had much to be encouraged by. I feel this team grew throughout the season and showed particular character and strength during the last three months of the campaign.

We were unbeaten in the last eleven games of the season and we must transfer that belief into the future.

We began the new season by welcoming four new players into the squad, including Mathieu Flamini who rejoins us, and German international midfielder Mesut Ozil – a top quality player who is a fantastic addition to the squad.

I want to thank all of our wonderful fans for the amazing support you give us throughout the year. I speak for all at the Club when I say it means a great deal to us and makes all the difference to the players on the pitch.

I hope you enjoy the Official Arsenal Annual 2014 and I thank you again for your continued support.

See you at Emirates,

Arsène Wenger

Premier League Review 2012-13

A season that started slowly soon sprang to life as exciting new star signings such as Cazorla, Giroud and Podolski adapted to the Premier League and began to show the fans what they could do. At the turn of the year the Gunners went on a run of impressive performances and memorable wins that would eventually secure them a UEFA Champions League place once again. Here follows the story of 2012/13 in the league...

August

The opening month of the Premier League campaign began with some impressive debuts and tell-tale signs of great things to come. First up at Emirates Stadium were Sunderland in a game that ended in a goalless draw but wasn't without plenty of chances. Abou Diaby and new signing Lukas Podolski were both unlucky to see their shots well saved, while the fans were in raptures at their first viewing of Santi Cazorla, making a lively start in an Arsenal shirt.

The Gunners were also held to a draw at Stoke City's Britannia Stadium. This time it was new French striker Olivier Giroud – making his first full start – who stood out. Along with Podolski and Cazorla, Giroud caused the home side problems throughout the game but couldn't convert chances into goals. Vito Mannone put in a solid performance when Stoke did threaten the Arsenal goal. Giroud came closest to breaking the deadlock in the final minutes with a left-foot strike that just went over the bar. After 180 minutes of League football Arsenal fans had witnessed some promising performances from new stars in the making but were still desperate to see some goals.

18th	Arsenal **0-0** Sunderland	
26th	Stoke City **0-0** Arsenal	

September

That desire for goals was certainly fulfilled in September with a fine run of Premier League and cup victories that kicked off with a rousing win over Liverpool in their own back yard. Lukas Podolski got off the mark with his and Arsenal's first Premier League goal for 2012/13 and Santi Cazorla silenced the Kop and bagged all three points with a strike that was too hot for Pepe Reina to handle.

Two weeks later Arsenal smashed Southampton at Emirates Stadium. The Gunners were gifted with an early own goal before Podolski fired in a free-kick to make it two-nil after 31 minutes. A first goal of the season for Gervinho followed by another gift from the shaky Saints defence saw the Gunners go in at half-time with a 4-1 lead. Gervinho struck again, latching on to a smart pass from Aaron Ramsey midway through the second half before Theo Walcott made it six in the last minute of the game.

It was a different story for Arsenal when they travelled up to face the Champions, Manchester City. A battling performance saw the Gunners bounce back from being a goal down to earn a draw via an unlikely source – a rocket shot from Laurent Koscielny. A month that had started so well ended on a sour note at home to London rivals Chelsea. Despite a fourth goal of the season for Gervinho, the Gunners' slick passing game was snuffed out by a determined opposition.

October

Another month, another London derby and another headline-grabbing display from Santi Cazorla. The Gunners did go a goal down early on at West Ham, but Giroud levelled the scores just before the half-time whistle. Theo Walcott then turned the game around – firing home an assist from Giroud – before Cazorla capped a man-of-the-match performance with a wonderful left-foot finish from 25 yards out.

The return of Jack Wilshere from injury to the subs bench for the away trip to Norwich City was one of few highlights in a disappointing defeat. Wilshere did start against QPR where only an inspired performance from Julio Cesar in the Rangers' goal kept the visitors in the game. Bacary Sagna also began his first game since May and supplied a clever cross to Aaron Ramsey whose header hit the crossbar. The Gunners pummelled the opponent's goal throughout but it wasn't until six minutes from time that Mikel Arteta finally broke the deadlock with a scrappy but deserved winner.

6th   **West Ham 1-3 Arsenal**
(Giroud, Walcott, Cazorla)

20th   **Norwich City 1-0 Arsenal**

27th   **Arsenal 1-0 QPR**
(Arteta)

November

November featured mixed fortunes for Arsenal against two of their biggest rivals. It began with a defeat at Old Trafford. Former fans' favourite Robin van Persie put United ahead and the home side went two-up before Arsenal were dealt a crushing blow when Jack Wilshere was shown a second yellow card. Cazorla struck again in injury time but it was too little too late.

Gunners fans then witnessed a six-goal see-saw game at home to Fulham. Arsenal went two up through Giroud and Podolski but the west Londoners hit back to lead by three goals to two. Giroud struck again to make it 3-3 and Arsenal were handed the chance to kill the tie in injury time but Arteta saw his penalty saved.

Arch rivals Spurs came to Emirates Stadium and grabbed an early goal through Adebeyor – but it wasn't enough to hinder a storming performance from Arsenal and Cazorla in particular. Adebeyor saw red as Arsenal went on the rampage, thrashing Spurs 5-2 in a dramatic derby that included Per Mertesacker's first goal in English football.

The month ended with two more points from hard-earned draws at Aston Villa on a rain-swept night in the Midlands and at Goodison Park. The Everton game was the more entertaining with Walcott putting Arsenal ahead after just 52 seconds and both teams' goalkeepers having busy nights.

3rd	**Manchester United 2-1 Arsenal**	
	(Cazorla)	
10th	**Arsenal 3-3 Fulham**	
	(Giroud (2), Podolski)	
17th	**Arsenal 5-2 Tottenham Hotspur**	
	(Mertesacker, Podolski, Giroud, Cazorla, Walcott)	
24th	**Aston Villa 0-0 Arsenal**	
28th	**Everton 1-1 Arsenal**	
	(Walcott)	

December

Arsenal's League form stammered again with a late defeat at home to Swansea. Wojciech Szczesny excelled to keep Swansea's marauding Spaniard, Michu, at bay in the first half, and the Gunners looked much livelier in attack after half time. Just as the game seemed to be destined for a draw Michu struck twice in the final two minutes to steal all three points.

But it was back to winning ways when West Brom came to Emirates Stadium one week later. Arteta buried two penalties to reignite the push for a Champions League spot and December continued to be the season of good cheer for Gunners fans with a 5-2 thumping of Reading. Another memorable performance from Cazorla was marked with his first hat-trick in English football while Podolski and Walcott also got on the scoresheet.

A hard-fought win against Wigan – secured by another Arteta penalty – was followed by the visit of Newcastle for what proved to be a 10-goal thriller. Struggling Newcastle failed to cope with Theo Walcott – playing as the lead striker – and the England international grabbed a hat-trick. Two more from Giroud and a first League strike of the season for Alex Oxlade-Chamberlain ensured the supporters would see the New Year in with plenty of cheer!

1st   Arsenal 0-2 Swansea City

8th   Arsenal 2-0 West Brom
        (Arteta (2))

17th   Reading 2-5 Arsenal
        (Podolski, Cazorla (3), Walcott)

22nd   Wigan Athletic 0-1 Arsenal
        (Arteta)

29th   Arsenal 7-3 Newcastle Utd
        (Walcott(3), Oxlade-Chamberlain, Podolski, Giroud)

January

The New Year began with a tough away draw at Southampton. A red card for Koscielny after just nine minutes at home to Manchester City meant Arsenal were left chasing the game and slipped to their fifth League defeat of the season.

Again early set-backs in the next match, away to Chelsea, meant the Gunners gave themselves a mountain to climb. Two-nil down after just 16 minutes, Arsène Wenger's men never gave in and although Walcott grabbed his 15th goal of the campaign, they couldn't find that elusive equaliser.

Things didn't look any better when West Ham took a shock early lead at Emirates Stadium three days later. But this time it only served to rattle the cage of a raging Red Army. Giroud equalised within four minutes and after Wenger worked his magic during the break the Gunners went on the rampage in the second half – scoring four more thanks to an outstanding performance from Lukas Podolski.

Arsenal succumbed to an early goal again, this time at home to Liverpool and when the visitors doubled their lead on 60 minutes all looked lost. But Giroud nodded in his 14th goal of the season five minutes later and Walcott pulled things level. Giroud then came close to seizing a victory against all odds in the dying minutes but saw his shot trickle wide.

1st   **Southampton 1-1 Arsenal**
        (Do Prado (og))

13th   **Arsenal 0-2 Manchester City**

20th   **Chelsea 2-1 Arsenal**
        (Walcott)

23rd   **Arsenal 5-1 West Ham**
        (Podolski, Giroud (2), Cazorla, Walcott)

30th   **Arsenal 2-2 Liverpool**
        (Giroud, Walcott)

February

February on the other hand was a magnificent month in the League with three wins out of three. It began with the visit of a typically resilient Stoke City and a goalkeeper – Asmir Begovic – in top form. But Lukas Podolski came off the bench to breach the deep-lying defence to win the game.

The omens weren't good for the trip to Sunderland as injuries meant Bacary Sagna was forced to play as an emergency centre half. But Cazorla snatched what would be the winning goal in the first half and the Gunners held out despite having Carl Jenkinson sent off with 30 minutes still to play.

Cazorla was on fire once more for the visit of Aston Villa. The Spaniard bagged both goals in a win that meant the Gunners had now taken 13 points from a potential 15 in the League. This run highlighted a positive change in form for Arsenal, and Cazorla's early strike for his first goal was yet more reason to celebrate at Emirates Stadium.

2nd   Arsenal **1-0** Stoke City
(Podolski)

9th   Sunderland **0-1** Arsenal
(Cazorla)

23rd   Arsenal **2-1** Aston Villa
(Cazorla (2))

March

The free flowing football Arsenal were playing continued as they took on their North London neighbours. But two shock strikes, against the run of play, meant Spurs went in at half-time in the lead. Per Mertesacker gave the Gunners hope when he headed home a Walcott free-kick and despite even Szczesny joining the attack at the death Tottenham held out to take all three points.

The Reds sought revenge on their trip to Swansea and secured it with a two-nil win that featured a first goal for January signing Nacho Monreal. The Spanish fullback put in a dogged performance that was typical of the team's display that day and Gervinho sealed the victory in injury time.

The Ivorian was also on target again when Reading came to Emirates later that month. Once again the Berkshire side were on the end of a crushing display from a fired-up Gunners side. Cazorla and Giroud put the Reds three up before Robson-Kanu clawed one back for the visitors. But Arsenal dominated the game and skipper Arteta wrapped it up with a penalty 13 minutes from time.

3rd   **Tottenham Hotspur 2-1 Arsenal**
(Mertesacker)

16th   **Swansea City 0-2 Arsenal**
(Monreal, Gervinho)

30th   **Arsenal 4-1 Reading**
(Gervinho, Cazorla, Giroud, Arteta)

April

With the battle for a UEFA Champions League spot being fiercely contested and only six weeks of the season left every point earned was vital. Tomas Rosicky gave the Gunners a two-nil lead over West Brom at the Hawthorns which proved crucial to secure victory – especially after Mertesacker saw red in the 70th minute and a 10-man Arsenal had to dig deep to stop the Baggies snatching a draw.

It was that never-say-die attitude that came to the Gunners' aid in the home tie against Norwich. The visitors nicked a lead on 56 minutes and Arsène Wenger responded by bringing on Walcott and Podolski. The resultant pressure led to panic in the Norwich defence – conceding a penalty which Arteta converted in the 85th minute. Giroud hit a second three minutes later and Podolski's sweet strike in injury time marked an incredible turnaround.

Everton proved to be even tougher opposition in the next home fixture and an intense, tight game ended with the spoils shared. Fulham proved to be equally combative opponents four days later – though possibly too much for their own good. They were down to 10 men after just 12 minutes and their frailty was exposed when Mertesacker scored the winner.

Theo Walcott silenced the cheers of newly crowned champions Manchester United when he struck the first blow after only two minutes of the home tie. But United managed to grab a point when Van Persie went to ground after a challenge from Bacary Sagna and converted the penalty he'd won.

6th	West Brom **0-2** Arsenal	
	(Rosicky (2))	
13th	Arsenal **3-1** Norwich City	
	(Arteta, Giroud, Podolski)	
16th	Arsenal **0-0** Everton	
20th	Fulham **0-1** Arsenal	
	(Mertesacker)	
28th	Arsenal **1-1** Manchester United	
	(Walcott)	

May

With just three games to go Arsenal's hopes of making the UEFA Champions League for a 16th consecutive season were on a knife edge. Wins were essential to keep up the pressure on both Spurs and Chelsea who were also toughing it out for the third and fourth spots. The final month couldn't have got off to a better start when Walcott fired home the fastest League goal of the season after just 20 seconds of the trip to Loftus Road, which was enough to defeat QPR.

The visit of Wigan Athletic – a team fighting for their survival in the top flight – was potentially more of a challenge. But Arsenal's outstanding form in the League – just one defeat in their last 14 games – was emphatically summed up in the last 45 minutes. Podolski eased any initial nerves with a goal after just 11 minutes. The visitors pulled things level just before half-time, then Walcott put the Reds ahead after the break and Podolski added his second before Aaron Ramsey sealed the points and in doing so confirmed Wigan's relegation to the Championship.

For the final game away to Newcastle United the Gunners knew that anything less than a win could hand their Champions League spot to Spurs. It lead to an edgy, nervous performance at times but when Koscielny connected with Walcott's free kick on 52 minutes, he also ensured that Arsenal would compete in Europe's premier club competition next season at the expense of their bitterest rivals.

4th	QPR 0-1 Arsenal
	(Walcott)
14th	Arsenal 4-1 Wigan Athletic
	(Podolski (2), Walcott, Ramsey)
19th	Newcastle United 0-1 Arsenal
	(Koscielny)

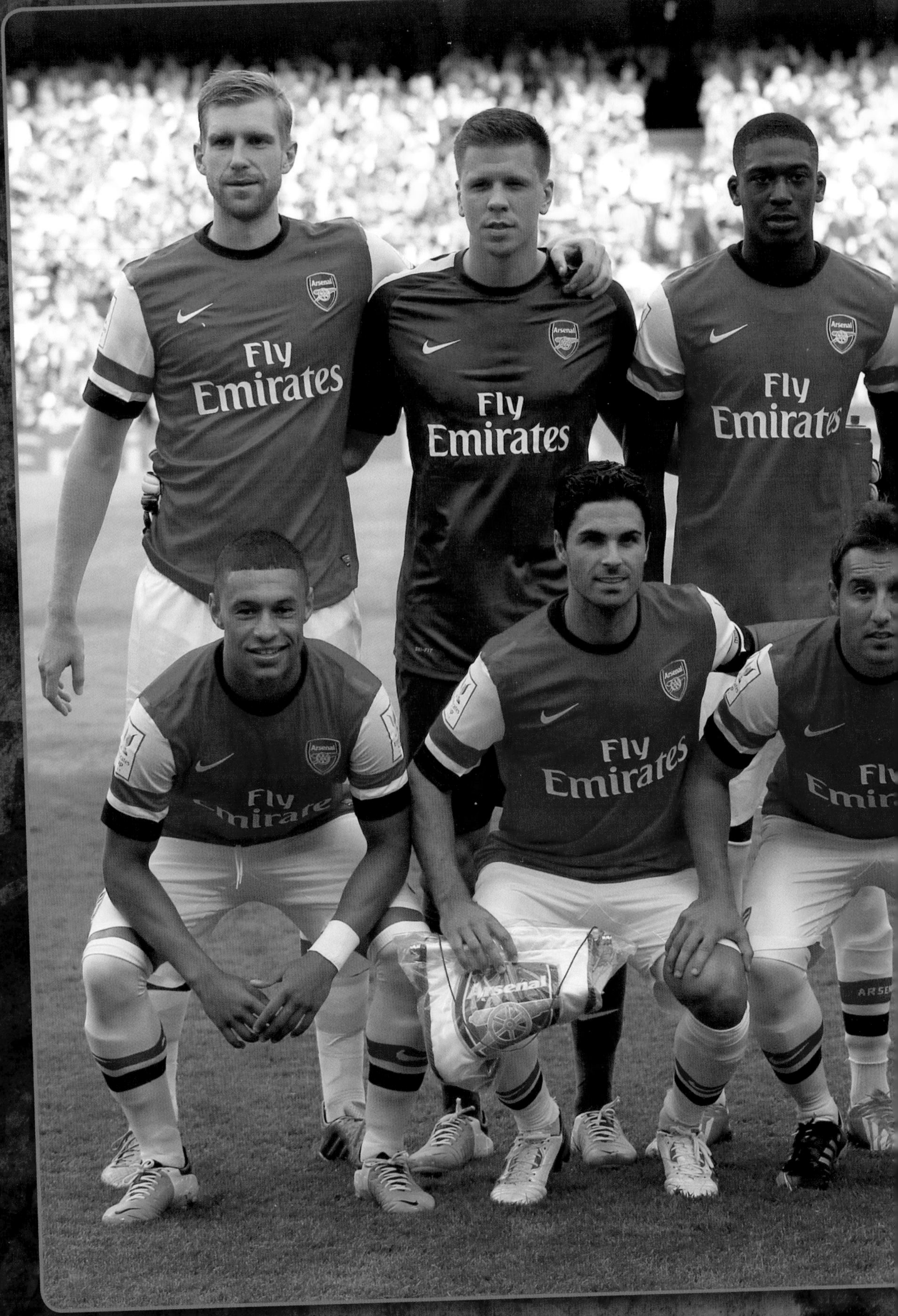
Fly
Emirates
Fly
Emirates
Fly
Emirates
Fly
Emirates
Arsenal

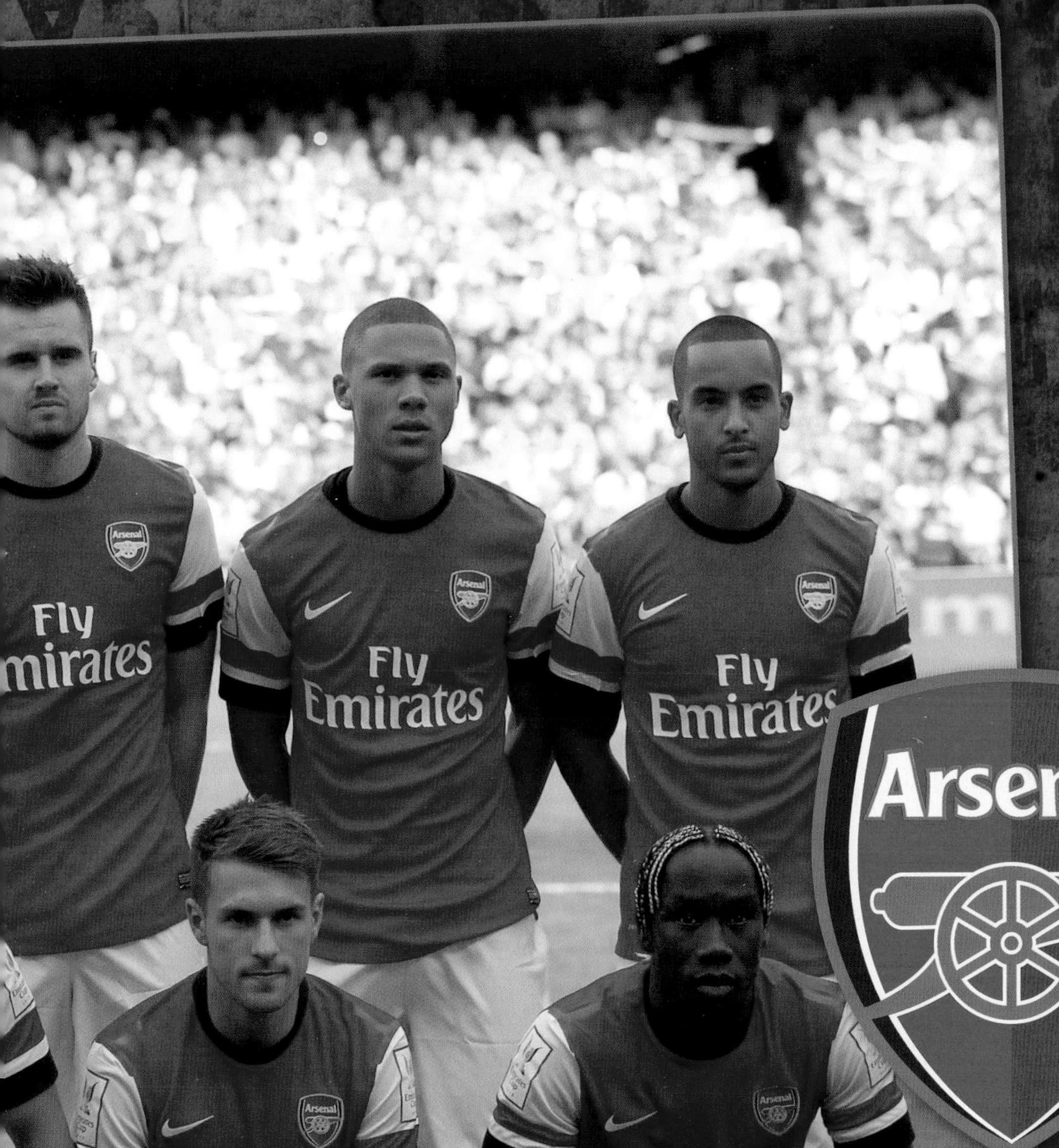
Fly Emirates

UEFA CHAMPIONS LEAGUE REVIEW

2012/13

Montpellier v Arsenal

The Gunners grabbed a crucial 2-1 victory in Montpellier on the opening night of their UEFA Champions League Group B campaign. Having fallen behind on nine minutes, the Gunners sealed the win with two goals in swift succession. Lukas Podolski finished clinically on 16 minutes and Gervinho swept home Carl Jenkinson's cross two minutes later.

18 September, 2012

Montpellier 1-2 Arsenal

(Podolski 16, Gervinho 18)

Euro fact: The win stretched Arsenal's unbeaten record away from home against French teams to nine games, a record that began in the mid-1990s!

Arsenal v Olympiacos

A hard-fought 3-1 win over Olympiacos took Wenger's team one step closer to qualification from Group B. Goals from Gervinho, Podolski and Ramsey were more than enough to cancel out Mitroglou's strike, which came on the brink of half time. Meanwhile, Schalke and Montpellier drew 2-2 in Germany, sending the Gunners clear at the top of Group B.

3 October, 2012

Arsenal 3-1 Olympiacos

(Gervinho 42, Podolski 56, Ramsey 90)

Euro fact: This was the third visit of Olympiacos to Emirates Stadium in four seasons.

Arsenal v Schalke 04

Two late goals from the German side dealt Arsenal their first European defeat of the season. Klaas-Jan Huntelaar, who had scored Emirates Stadium's first ever goal in 2006, opened the scoring on 76 minutes, before Ibrahim Afellay added another with just four minutes left. Arsenal had enjoyed plenty of possession but clever counter-attacking from the visitors won the day.

24 October, 2012

Arsenal 0-2 Schalke 04

Euro fact: This was Arsenal's first defeat to foreign opposition on home soil for 45 games.

Schalke 04 v Arsenal

Arsenal looked good for a vital away win when first-half goals from Theo Walcott and Oliver Giroud took them into the break 2-1 ahead. However, Jefferson Farfan equalised just past the hour mark as the home side improved. Walcott, whose opener was grabbed from close range, nearly sealed a win late on, but the Gunners had to content themselves with a draw.

6 November, 2012

Schalke 04 2-2 Arsenal

(Walcott 18, Giroud 26)

Euro fact: It was Walcott's 50th goal in his 233rd appearance for the Club

GROUP B							
Schalke	6	3	3	0	10	6	+4	12
Arsenal	6	3	1	2	10	8	+2	10
Olympiacos	6	3	0	3	9	9	0	9
Montpellier	6	0	2	4	6	12	-6	2

Arsenal v Montpellier

Goals from Jack Wilshere and Lukas Podolski handed Arsenal a victory which sent them through the group stage of the UEFA Champions League. Wilshere's strike, his first for 725 days, opened the scoring early in the second half. It was Podolski who delivered the pick of the goals, his thunderous volley following a fine assist from Olivier Giroud.

21 November, 2012

Arsenal 2-0 Montpellier

(Wilshere 49, Podolski 63)

Euro fact: Jernade Meade, 20, was given his full Gunners debut at left-back and five teenagers were named on the substitutes' bench against Olympiacos.

Olympiacos v Arsenal

The Gunners concluded their UEFA Champions League Group B campaign with a disappointing 2-1 defeat at Olympiacos. The opener from in-form Tomas Rosicky was cancelled out by two second-half strikes from the home side. This meant the Club finished in second place in the Group. However, the important fact was that they had qualified for the next stage.

4 December, 2012

Olympiacos 2-1 Arsenal

(Rosciky 83)

Euro fact: This was the 13th successive season in which the Club progressed to the group stage of the Champions League.

Arsenal v Bayern Munich

Arsène Wenger's side were beaten 3-1 by the Germans in the first leg of this last-16 tie. Toni Kroos and Thomas Muller gave the visitors a fine first-half lead. Although Lukas Podolski reduced the deficit 10 minutes after the restart, Mario Mandzukic restored the Germans' two-goal buffer, leaving the Gunners with it all to do in the second leg.

19 February, 2013

Arsenal 1-3 Bayern Munich

(Podolski 54)

Bayern Munich v Arsenal

A 2-0 victory at the home of German giants Bayern Munich should be an occasion of joy and pride for any European team, yet for the Gunners it was a bittersweet moment. Goals from Olivier Giroud and Laurent Koscielny were not enough to avoid elimination from the competition due to the away goal rule.

13 March, 2013

Bayern Munich 0-2 Arsenal

(Giroud 3, Koscielny 86)

Euro fact: Bayern, who had been beaten in the previous season's final, went on to win the 2012/13 UEFA Champions League.

Euro fact: This was Lukasz Fabianski's first start in a year.

PLAYER PROFILES

Arsenal

KIERAN GIBBS

BORN: SEPTEMBER 26, 1989, LAMBETH, LONDON

POSITION: DEFENDER

SQUAD NUMBER: 28

PREVIOUS CLUB(S): WIMBLEDON, NORWICH CITY (LOAN)

ARSENAL DEBUT: OCTOBER 31, 2007

The lowdown: Kieran, who has been with Arsenal since 2004, started life as a winger. He moved to left back following a loan spell at Norwich City. The Londoner has superb pace, anticipation and technique, qualities which have continued to develop each year. He has featured twice for England, against Hungary and France.

ARSÈNE WENGER SAYS:

" October and November was really a springboard for him where he moved forward. He's a candidate for higher up. "

RANDOM FACT: Kieran made his 100th Arsenal appearance when he came on as a substitute against Reading in March 2013.

LAURENT KOSCIELNY

BORN: SEPTEMBER 10, 1985, TULLE, FRANCE

POSITION: DEFENDER

SQUAD NUMBER: 6

PREVIOUS CLUB(S): EN AVANT GUINGAMP, TOURS, LORIENT

ARSENAL DEBUT: AUGUST 15, 2010

The lowdown: From the moment he set foot in the Club, the Frenchman has boosted Arsenal with his pace, athleticism and speedy reactions. He is also a formidable foe in one-on-one duels. After a solid first year with the Gunners, Laurent has grown in stature and popularity each season. A year after signing for Arsenal he received his first international call-up and is now a France regular.

ARSÈNE WENGER SAYS:

" Laurent is one of Europe's finest defenders. "

RANDOM FACT: Prior to turning out for France, Laurent was also eligible to play for Poland.

MIKEL ARTETA

BORN: MARCH 26, 1982, SAN SEBASTIAN, SPAIN

POSITION: MIDFIELDER

SQUAD NUMBER: 8

PREVIOUS CLUB(S): EVERTON, REAL SOCIEDAD, RANGERS, PSG (LOAN), BARCELONA

ARSENAL DEBUT: SEPTEMBER 10, 2011

The lowdown: He arrived at the Club just hours before the transfer deadline ran out in August 2011 – and midfield maestro Mikel has proved a shrewd deal ever since. The Spaniard is one of the English game's most professional and consistent players. Although a deeply creative player at heart, he has also contributed additional solidity to the Arsenal teams he has graced. The former Everton, Rangers and Barcelona star is class personified, on and off the pitch.

ARSÈNE WENGER SAYS:

"He could be a good poker player. He is a winner. He is ready to fight to win."

RANDOM FACT: Mikel was named the Toffees' Player of the Year three times.

JACK WILSHERE

BORN: JANUARY 01, 1992, STEVENAGE, HERTFORDSHIRE

POSITION: MIDFIELDER

SQUAD NUMBER: 10

PREVIOUS CLUB(S): BOLTON (LOAN)

ARSENAL DEBUT: SEPTEMBER 13, 2008

The lowdown: One of the most exciting England players of his generation, Jack has been with the Club since the age of nine and was a pivotal member of the 2009 FA Youth Cup-winning side. Since joining the senior side his progress has been exceptional. He won the PFA Young Player of the Year award in his debut campaign and is now one of Europe's most admired midfielders.

RANDOM FACT: In 2011, Jack became an ambassador for St John Ambulance.

ARSÈNE WENGER SAYS:

"He is naturally a guy who is not scared of anything on the football pitch and that is usually the sign of a leader."

PLAYER PROFILES

RANDOM FACT: His full name is Santiago Cazorla González.

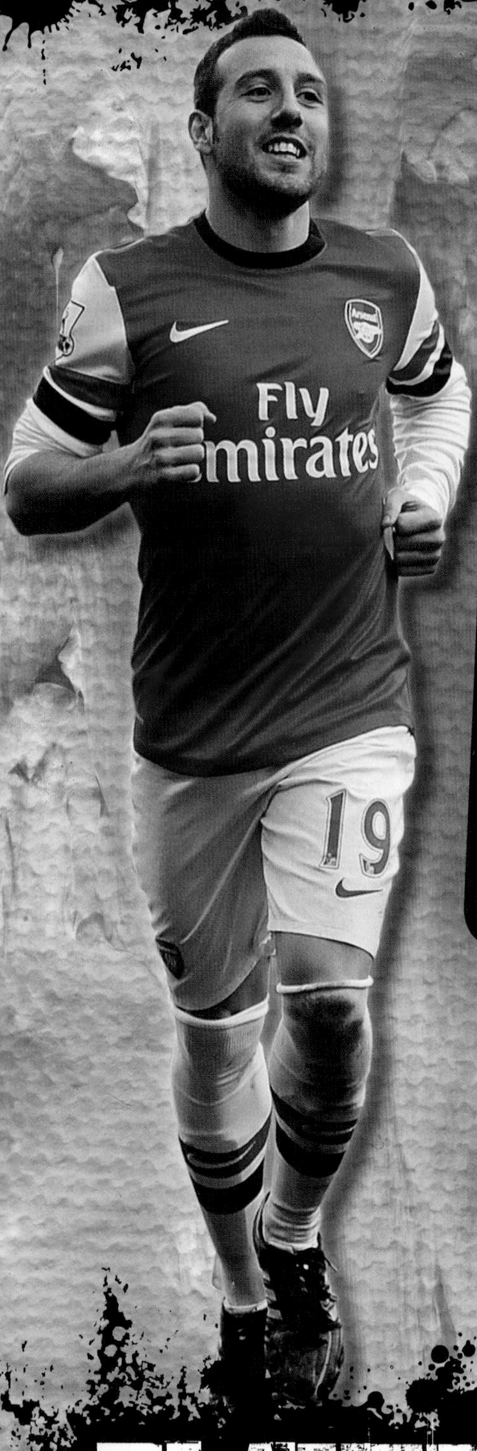

SANTI CAZORLA

BORN:	DECEMBER 13, 1984, LLANERA, SPAIN
POSITION:	MIDFIELDER
SQUAD NUMBER:	19
PREVIOUS CLUB(S):	MALAGA, VILLARREAL, RECREATIVO, VILLARREAL, OVIEDO
ARSENAL DEBUT:	AUGUST 18, 2012

The lowdown: A cultured, versatile and attacking midfielder, Santi Cazorla joined Arsenal from Malaga in August, 2012. Making 47 starts in his first season in north London, he became a hugely popular Gooner. The Spaniard is suited to either wing or a central role, and has been a regular for Spain for four years, a member of his country's victorious squads at the European Championship in 2008 and 2012.

ARSÈNE WENGER SAYS:

"He is right-footed but when you watch him play you don't know. It shows how important that is in the modern midfield."

PLAYER PROFILES

OLIVIER GIROUD

BORN: SEPTEMBER 30, 1986, CHAMBERY, FRANCE

POSITION: STRIKER

SQUAD NUMBER: 12

PREVIOUS CLUB(S): GRENOBLE, ISTRES (LOAN), TOURS, MONTPELLIER

ARSENAL DEBUT: AUGUST 18, 2012

The lowdown: Scoring 17 goals in just 33 starts, Olivier has proved to be a fine addition to the Arsenal squad. Joining from French champions Montpellier, he immediately showed his quick feet, intelligent running, deadly finishing ability and a willingness to involve himself fully in build-up play. A regular for France, he is now one of Europe's most feared forwards.

RANDOM FACT: He made his international debut against the United States in November 2011 on the same night as future Gunners team-mate Laurent Koscielny.

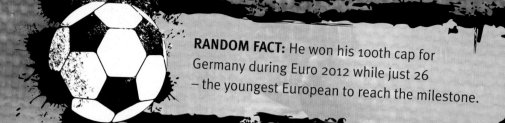

LUKAS PODOLSKI

BORN: JUNE 04, 1985, GLIWICE, POLAND

POSITION: STRIKER

SQUAD NUMBER: 9

PREVIOUS CLUB(S): COLOGNE, BAYERN MUNICH, COLOGNE

ARSENAL DEBUT: AUGUST 18, 2012

The lowdown: Lukas has always been a prolific goalscorer: he scored 51 goals in his first 85 games for Cologne and has a strong record at international level for Germany. With pace, skill and a clinical left foot, Lukas has settled into the Premier League well. He scored 16 times in 33 starts during his debut Arsenal season and supported his team-mates' efforts throughout the pitch with his versatile and enthusiastic play.

ARSÈNE WENGER SAYS:

" He has a fantastic left foot – you saw that on his goal. The quality of his crosses is absolutely immaculate and when you play in the middle, you want people who can cross like him. "

ALEX OXLADE-CHAMBERLAIN

BORN: AUGUST 15, 1993, PORTSMOUTH, HAMPSHIRE

POSITION: STRIKER

SQUAD NUMBER: 15

PREVIOUS CLUB(S): SOUTHAMPTON

ARSENAL DEBUT: AUGUST 28, 2011

The lowdown: A promising young English forward joining the Club from Southampton, Alex followed in the footsteps of team-mate Theo Walcott as he signed for the Gunners in 2011. The following year, he came into his own. A sturdy, entertaining talent with outstanding vision and the ability to play in wide or central areas, he is now a fan's favourite. With a strong sense that the best is yet to come, the future is bright for player and Club.

PLAYER PROFILES

ARSÈNE WENGER SAYS:

" Alex is a versatile player who can play in a number of positions. He can play as an attacking centre midfielder, or wide left and right. He is a perceptive passer of the ball and has a great understanding of the game. "

RANDOM FACT: Alex is the son of former England winger Mark Chamberlain.

THE FA CUP

Although Arsenal's FA Cup campaign did not end in silverware, it included plenty of incident and goals. Two of the four ties were classic see-saw encounters with the lead changing hands, while the remainder were tight nail-biters. Here are all the details you need to know about the Club's 2012/13 FA Cup run. We look forward to more cup drama in 2014!

3rd Round, Away v Swansea City

After a gentle first-half this tie erupted into drama in the second period. After Swansea took the lead just before the hour mark, the scoreline swung back and forth before ending all-square. Swansea substitute Michu opened the scoring minutes after joining the action. Then, two goals in three minutes swung the pendulum the way of the Gunners. First, Lukas Podolski twisted and fired low into the bottom corner with nine minutes remaining on the clock. Then, defender Kieran Gibbs smashed a sweet volley into the roof of the net to put his side ahead. However, with four minutes left, Danny Graham swept home an equaliser. But for the fine form of Swansea goalkeeper Michael Vorm, the Gunners would have won the tie comfortably.

Match fact: Swansea defender Kyle Bartley was part of the Arsenal team that won the FA Youth Cup in 2009.

3rd Round, Home v Swansea City

Man of the Match Jack Wilshere struck a deserved winner minutes from the end of a tie in which Wenger's team created no less than 26 goalscoring chances. On a cold north London night, Walcott hit the woodwork and Giroud saw an effort blocked on the line. It made for agonising viewing for both sets of fans, as the visitors created fine goalscoring chances themselves. Finally, with five minutes left, Cazorla nudged the ball to Giroud, whose flick set up Wilshere to slam the ball home from just outside the area. Victory belonged to the Gunners!

Match fact: Wilshere's winner was his fifth goal in 80 appearances for Arsenal.

4th Round, Away v Brighton

Theo Walcott pounced five minutes from time to win a thrilling FA Cup tie at Brighton and send the Gunners into the fifth round. His deflected shot handed Wenger's team a deserved victory after they had led twice through a brace from Giroud. Headers from Ashley Barnes and Leonardo Ulloa had leveled the scoreline, raising the prospect of another replay. Then, Wenger sent on Gibbs, Wilshere and Walcott to shake things up. The pick of Giroud's brace was his opener, which was a beauty of a curled shot into the top corner, following fine work from Rosicky and Podolski. Walcott's winner, deflected by El-Abd, was no less valuable. Arsenal were through!

Match fact: Olivier Giroud was named Man of the Match by Arsenal fans – 85% of them chose him for the honour!

Match fact: This was Arsenal's first home defeat in this competition for 35 matches – a record going back to 1997.

5th Round, Home v Blackburn Rovers

For the second cup-tie running, Arsène Wenger chose to send on his big guns in the second half. Yet just seconds after he introduced Jack Wilshere, Santi Cazorla and Theo Walcott, the Gunners fell behind, thanks to a goal from Colin Kazim-Richards. In the remaining 19 minutes, Arsenal attacked ferociously in search of a goal, but Blackburn Rovers goalkeeper Jake Kean pulled off some crucial saves. The match ended with vastly differing emotions than those governing Blackburn's previous visit to Emirates, which had seen Arsenal win 7-1. This time, the Gunners lost. Their FA Cup campaign was over.

REDS REWIND!

Let's step back in time and recall five famous victories from the Gunners vaults.

Which are your favourite games of yesteryear?

1

Arsenal 7-1 Blackburn Rovers
February 4, 2012

Take a Robin van Persie hat-trick, two goals from Alex Oxlade-Chamberlain, add a strike from Mikel Arteta strike and late goal from Thierry Henry and you have a thumping victory against Blackburn Rovers. Nice.

2

Tottenham Hotspur 2-2 Arsenal
April 25, 2004

Arsenal won the Premiership title thanks to the point earned at the home of their rivals. On target for the Gunners were Patrick Vieira and Robert Pires.

3

Real Madrid 0-1 Arsenal
February 21, 2006

The Gunners became the first English side to beat the Spanish giants on their own patch. A delicious goal from Thierry Henry two minutes after the interval was enough to secure this famous and historic victory.

Inter Milan 1-5 Arsenal
November 25, 2003

Thierry Henry was influential as the Club inflicted Inter's heaviest home defeat in 47 years of European football. The half-time scoreline was 1-1. In the second-half the Gunners opened the floodgates and built a comfortable victory.

4

Manchester United 0-1 Arsenal
May 8, 2002

Some 12 minutes into the second half of this tie, Sylvain Wiltord scored the game's only goal, sealing the Premiership title – and the Double – for the Gunners. The visiting fans waved a 'Champions Section' banner.

5

DID YOU KNOW?

Here are some dazzling facts about the Club that you may – or may not – be aware of...

- It took Arsène Wenger just 398 matches to collect 200 wins as Gunners boss.

- In May 2013, Lukas Podolski scored Germany's fastest ever goal in their 4-2 win against Ecuador.

- The most common scoreline during season 2012/13 was 1-0.

- In October 2004, Manager Arsène Wenger was awarded the Freedom of the Borough of Islington.

- Santi Cazorla was the only member of the squad to appear in every Premier League match in the 2012/13 season.

- The first and 50th matches at Emirates Stadium were both against Aston Villa – and both ended in 1-1 draws.

- Former captain Tony Adams made 669 appearances for Arsenal.

- Arsenal had just £19 in its bank account when it moved to Arsenal Stadium in 1913.

- Arsène Wenger predicted that Bayern Munich would win the 2013 UEFA Champions League final.

- Over 60,000 cubic metres of concrete were used to build Emirates Stadium.

- Theo Walcott did not make his Arsenal debut until seven months after he had joined the Club.

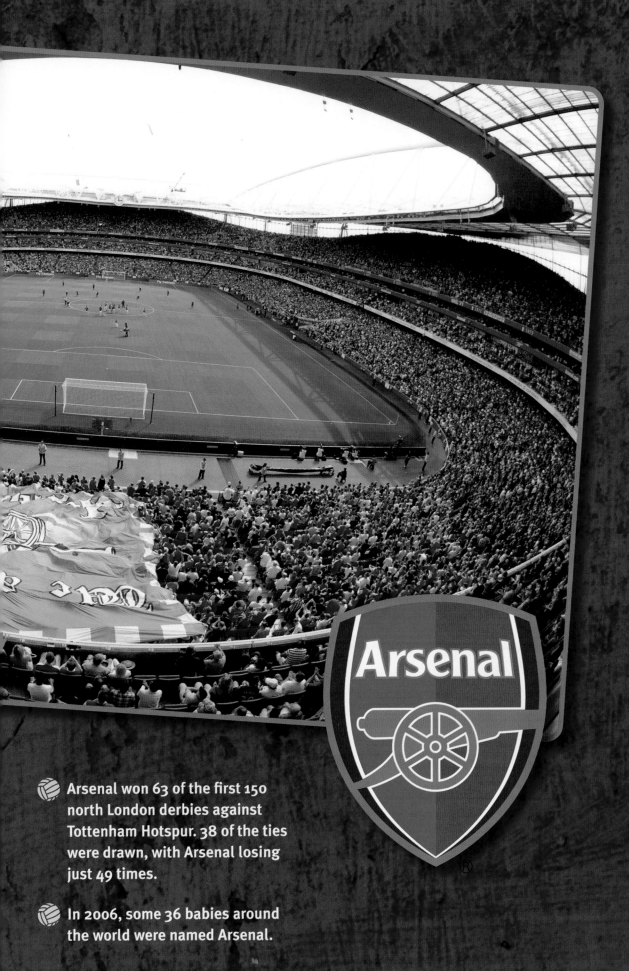

Arsenal won 63 of the first 150 north London derbies against Tottenham Hotspur. 38 of the ties were drawn, with Arsenal losing just 49 times.

In 2006, some 36 babies around the world were named Arsenal.

CAPITAL ONE CUP REVIEW
2012/13

In recent years the League cup has provided Arsenal with a testing ground to bring young talent on to a bigger stage and give fans a glimpse of stars in the making. This time around, Arsène Wenger took a different approach – combining established first-teamers and full internationals with the latest crop of promising youth-team and squad players. The result was a highly entertaining, goal-filled Capital One Cup run...

Arsenal v Coventry City

The Gunners set out their intentions from the very start of the competition with a line-up to face Coventry City that perfectly blended youth with experience. Many fans got a first glimpse of debutant goalkeeper Damian Martinez and defender Martin Angha – while midfielder Nico Yennaris was a mascot for Coventry's last visit to Arsenal in September 2000. It was mainly the 'veterans' who provided the firepower on this occasion though with Giroud, Arshavin and Theo Walcott among the scorers.

26 September, 2012
Arsenal 6-1 Coventry City
(Giroud, Oxlade-Chamberlain, Arshavin, Walcott (2), Miquel)

Reading v Arsenal

An absolutely amazing cup-tie at Reading's Madjeski Stadium began with Arsenal looking like they were crashing out after being 4-0 down by the 37th minute. The Gunners went in at half-time with only Theo Walcott's goal to show for their efforts. Then Giroud began to drive a belief that Arsenal weren't out of things when he made it 4-2 midway through the second half. Koscielny made it three to the Gunners with a minute to go before Walcott fired in a dramatic equaliser with just seconds remaining. Extra-time was just as heart-stopping with Chamakh putting Arsenal ahead, Reading pulling it back to 5-5 before Chamakh and finally Walcott sealed an incredible comeback.

30 October, 2012
Reading 5-7 Arsenal
(Walcott (3), Giroud, Koscielny, Chamakh (2))

Bradford City v Arsenal

Arsenal went behind again in their quarter-final tie at League Two Bradford in what would prove to be a much tighter game for the Gunners this time around. Wojciech Sczcesny was kept busy by the home side who took a lead on 16 minutes and fought doggedly to maintain it. Arsène Wenger changed the attacking line-up in the later stages – bringing on Rosicky, Oxlade-Chamberlain and Chamakh. Arsenal seized control of the game and skipper Vermaelen glanced in a header to force the game to extra-time. After 120 minutes the sides still couldn't be separated and it was down to spot kicks. But both Chamakh and Cazorla missed their penalties and when Vermaelen, the Arsenal hero of the night, hit the woodwork it sent the visitors out of the cup.

11 December, 2012
Bradford City 1-1 Arsenal
(Vermaelen) Bradford
win on penalties

TOP TEN

Arsenal's red-hot striker Theo Walcott has delighted fans with his stunning skills since he joined the Club in 2006. Here, we remember some of his finest moments for Club and country, as well as some admirable off-the-pitch endeavours!

THEO WALCOTT MOMENTS!

1 The Anfield assist

During the UEFA Champions League quarter-final at Liverpool in 2008, Theo received the ball on the edge of his own area. He then ran the length of the Anfield pitch, beating four defenders, and released the ball to Emmanuel Adebayor who slammed it home. Skill, pace, team-work and poise!

2 A towering hat-trick

Walcott was on unstoppable form against Blackpool in 2010. After opening the scoring on 13 minutes, he went on to score a hat-trick, and also set up chances for Andrey Arshavin and Marouane Chamakh. The third goal of Theo's trio was the best: Diaby was the provider for the Englishman to send the ball home in some style. Walcott and Arsenal at their best.

3 Opening his account

There are few better ways to break your goalscoring duck than against Chelsea in a cup final. In the 2007 Carling Cup Final, Theo received an inch-perfect pass from Abou Diaby, spun and then fired the ball into the far corner. He celebrated in style, running with his fist clenched, before he was mobbed by his delighted team-mates.

4 Three goals for the Three Lions

In September 2008, at just 19 years of age, Theo notched a stunning hat-trick for his country against Croatia. In doing so he became the youngest player to score a hat-trick for England. Bravo!

5 Joining the Gunners

Prior to him signing for the Club in 2006, Walcott was tracked by some of Europe's top clubs – at the tender age of 16, he was viewed as hot property by leading coaches. Showing he has good taste, he chose Arsenal FC – "a club I have admired for a long time".

6 International bright young thing

On 30 May, 2006, he became England's youngest ever player when he appeared against Hungary in a 3-1 friendly win at just 17 years and 75 days old.

7 20 seconds to comply

He scored the fastest goal of the 2012/13 season when he struck just 20 seconds into the tie against QPR. Walcott's strike, which took him to 20 for the season, also marked Arsenal's fastest Premier League goal of all time.

8 Derby delight

No Gunners fans will forget the 5-2 win over local rivals Tottenham in February 2012. Walcott struck twice as the team bounced back from a two-goal deficit to win handsomely.

9 Charity

Theo is a tireless ambassador for several charities including the Willow Foundation and the Arsenal Foundation. He has also represented charitable intiatives for a host of other good causes, including Centrepoint. He often visits sick children in hospital.

10 Here's to the future!

Gunners fans were delighted when, in January 2013, Theo signed a new long-term contract with the Club. Here's to the future!

FAMOUS FANS

From boxers, to rappers, comedians to presenters – here's a list of famous fans of the world's greatest team!

Dermot O'Leary
When it comes to Arsenal the presenter of the X Factor says 'it's a yes from me!'

Matt Lucas
The comedian has long been a Gooner and hoste The Arsenal Foundation Ball in 2013.

Dido
The songbird went to her first Arsenal match at the age of three!

Mo Farah
The double Olympic gold medallist often watches the team and has visited the training centre.

Davina McCall

Rachel Stevens

The former S-Club singer hopes Wenger's boys will reach for the stars!

Ian Poulter

The top-ranking golf legend often sings the praises of the Gunners on Twitter.

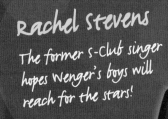

Chris Hollins

The father of the BBC presenter is former Arsenal star John Hollins MBE.

Audley Harrison

The former boxer loves it when the Gunners knockout the opposition!

Jay-Z

The rapper first became a Gunners fan when he saw Thierry Henry in action for the Club!

CROSSWORD

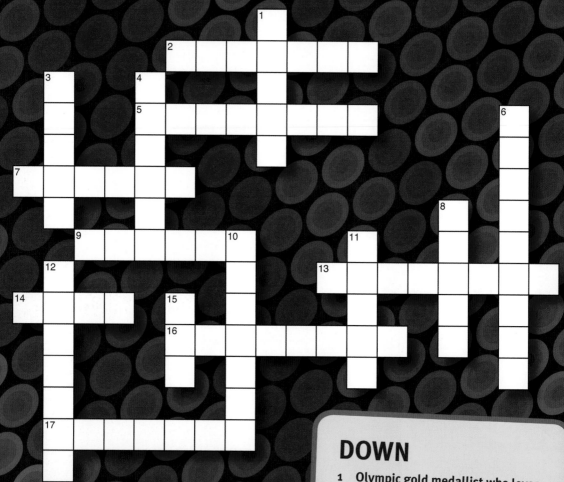

Answers on Page 61

ACROSS

2 A goal struck from 12 yards. (7)

5 Former Gunner Andrey's second name. (8)

7 The surname of the Club's boss. (6)

9 The name of the fan club is the _____ Gunners. (6)

13 Arsenal's home for 93 years. (8)

14 Arsenal's English midfield ace is _____ Wilshere. (4)

16 Where the Club lives. (8)

17 The Frenchman who holds the Club's scoring record is _____ Henry. (7)

DOWN

1 Olympic gold medallist who loves AFC is Mo _____ . (5)

3 The number of points gained for a win. (5)

4 The Gunners beat them 2-0 in Germany. _____ Munich. (6)

6 The Gunners love these. (9)

8 Every team wants to be top of the league _____ . (5)

10 Czech out this midfielder! (7)

11 The first name of our former Evertonian Spanish ace. (5)

12 He scored the first goal against Manchester City in the August 2013 friendly. (7)

15 It's where arsenal.com resides and where the ball needs to end up. (3)

SPOT THE BALL

Can you help Theo Walcott spot which is the real ball?

Answers on Page 61

The season in quotes

> 66 I have lost twice 7-1, once I lost 8-3 and once I won 9-3 and now 7-5. But this game was one I will remember always because it was from 4-0 down. 99

Andrey Arshavin after Arsenal beat Reading 7-5

> 66 We have players like Walcott, Podolski, Giroud and Cazorla who can score goals and that's what happened. 99

Wenger on a squad which shares the goalscoring burden

> 66 The big thing for us was getting that result at Bayern. I think we're more or less the only team that's won there this season so it just gives everybody a belief that we're doing alright. It was an important game for us. 99

Steve Bould on a turning point in Munich

> 66 The way the squad has stuck together this season and never given up is credit to them. 99

Kieran Gibbs on the character and spirit of the Gunners

> 66 I enjoy playing in that position a lot, I do – all the tackling and covering people and making the players around me better. I really enjoyed it this season. 99

Mikel Arteta on his new role at the base of the midfield

> 66 From the moment that I went out there, the fans were great. Even before the game when I was meeting Arsenal fans they were positive and all I can do now is prove to them that I can get back to the level I was at before and show them what I can do. 99

Jack Wilshere upon his much-anticipated return to first-team action

> 66 They've shown a combination of quality but attitude as well. In the modern day, I always admire the way they behaved and their focus every day in training. 99
>
> **Arsène Wenger on the squad**

> 66 It is difficult to play and block out that side of it, but I tried to do the best I could and hopefully everyone was happy with what I did. 99
>
> **Theo Walcott after signing a new long-term deal**

old school sayings

"I am going to make this the greatest Club in the world."

Herbert Chapman, on becoming Arsenal manager in 1925

"My aim is simple – to make Arsenal not just the best in the Premiership, but the biggest and best Club in the world."

Arsène Wenger echoes Chapman's theme in 1996

"I love wearing the Arsenal shirt and I get a very special feeling every time I put it on."

Thierry Henry

"I think without a doubt that Dennis Bergkamp is the greatest player to have played for Arsenal in the last 30 years."

Liam Brady

"I think we can go a whole season unbeaten."

Arsène Wenger in 2002. Two years later he was proved correct!

The season in numbers

Here is the story of season 2012/13 in numbers. From the top scorer, to the highest attendance, via the player who made the most clearances, this is a feast of football figures for every fan.

December was the month in which Arsenal scored most Premier League goals: they netted **15** times.

Olivier Giroud made the most substitute appearances, being sent on **14** times.

The Gunners scored 72 league goals – 6 more than Manchester City who finished two places higher in the table.

The Gunners' 10-goal aggregate scoreline, which came in the 7-3 win over Newcastle United, was only equalled on the final day, when West Bromwich Albion drew 5-5 with Manchester United.

Santi Cazorla made the most appearances, starting 47 matches and coming on as a substitute in two more.

Arsenal goalkeepers made 140 saves during the league campaign.

Arteta scored 5 of the 6 penalties he took. No player in the Premier League scored more from the penalty spot.

Per Mertesacker has made the highest number of clearances – 160.

The average attendance for home matches was 60079.

The Gunners were unbeaten for the final 10 league matches of the season...

Theo Walcott scored the campaign's fastest goal, netting after just 20 seconds at QPR in May.

...and in those games kept clean sheets in 5, and conceded only a single goal in the other 5.

Theo Walcott was top scorer with 21 goals.

The biggest away win was the 5-2 victory at Reading.

The season in stats

PLAYER	PREM LGE		EUROPE		FA CUP		LGE CUP		TOTAL	
	AP	GL	AP	GL	AP	GL	AP	GL	AP	GL
Wojciech Szczesny	25	0	3	0	4	0	1	0	33	0
Abou Diaby	10 + 1	0	1	0	3	0	0	0	14 + 1	0
Bacary Sagna	25	0	3	0	2	0	1	0	31	0
Per Mertesacker	33 + 1	3	6	0	3	0	1	0	43 + 1	3
Thomas Vermaelen	25 + 4	0	7	0	2	0	1	1	35 + 4	1
Laurent Koscielny	20 + 5	2	5	1	3	0	1	1	29 + 5	4
Tomas Rosicky	7 + 3	2	2 + 1	1	2	0	0 + 1	0	11 + 5	3
Mikel Arteta	34	6	7	0	2	0	0	0	43	6
Lukas Podolski	25 + 8	11	6	4	1 + 1	1	1	0	33 + 9	16
Jack Wilshere	20 + 5	0	3	1	2 + 2	1	1	0	26 + 7	2
Andre Santos	3 + 5	0	1 + 1	0	1	0	1	0	6 + 6	0
Emmanuel Frimpong	0	0	0	0	0	0	1 + 1	0	1 + 1	0
Olivier Giroud	24 + 10	11	4 + 3	2	4	2	1 + 1	2	33 + 14	17
Theo Walcott	24 + 8	14	3 + 2	1	2 + 2	1	2	5	31 + 12	21
Alex Oxlade-Chamberlain	11 + 14	1	3 + 1	0	2	0	1 + 1	1	17 + 16	2
Aaron Ramsey	21 + 15	1	4 + 3	1	2 + 1	0	1	0	28 + 19	2

PLAYER	PREM LGE		EUROPE		FA CUP		LGE CUP		TOTAL	
	AP	GL	AP	GL	AP	GL	AP	GL	AP	GL
Nacho Monreal	9 + 1	1	0	0	1	0	0	0	10 + 1	1
Sebastien Squillaci	0	0	1	0	0	0	0	0	1	0
Santi Cazorla	37 + 1	12	7	0	2 + 1	0	1	0	47 + 2	12
Johan Djourou	0	0	0	0	0	0	2	0	2	0
Lukasz Fabianski	4	0	1	0	0	0	0	0	5	0
Francis Coquelin	3 + 8	0	3 + 3	0	2	0	3	0	11 + 11	0
Andrey Arshavin	0 + 7	0	0 + 2	0	0	0	2	1	2 + 9	1
Vito Mannone	9	0	4	0	0	0	0	0	13	0
Carl Jenkinson	14	0	5	0	1	0	1	0	21	0
Gervinho	12 + 6	5	4 + 2	2	1	0	1	0	18 + 8	7
Kieran Gibbs	23 + 4	0	3	0	2 + 1	1	1	0	29 + 5	1
Marouane Chamakh	0	0	1	0	0	0	1 + 2	2	2 + 2	2
Martin Angha	0	0	0 + 1	0	0	0	1	0	1 + 1	0
Thomas Eisfeld	0	0	0	0	0	0	0 + 1	0	0 + 1	0
Serge Gnabry	0 + 1	0	0 + 1	0	0	0	1 + 1	0	1 + 3	0
Jernade Meade	0	0	1	0	0	0	0 + 1	0	1 + 1	0
Ignasi Miquel	0 + 1	0	0	0	0	0	2	1	2 + 1	1
Damian Martinez	0	0	0	0	0	0	2	0	2	0
Nico Yennaris	0	0	0	0	0	0	1	0	1	0

Junior Gunners

Catch up with recent highlights in the world of Junior Gunners – and find out how to join the fun!

The JG ball squad

A dedicated squad of 20 Junior Gunners helped to keep games flowing at Emirates Stadium.

Gunnersaurus' blog

Throughout the season, the Arsenal mascot kept the Junior Gunners entertained and informed with his blog, which took fans into the wonderful world of every Gooner's favourite dinosaur.

All aboard!

On Saturday, April 20, 40 lucky Junior Gunners were selected to travel along the Thames to Arsenal's game away at Fulham.

Chants would be a fine thing!

The JG launched a 'Fan Chant' competition, which was won by Junior Gunner Phoebe's Wojciech Szczesny-inspired chant 'They call me Szczesny'. Phoebe, aged 10, was given two match tickets for a home match and was also presented with a signed picture from Arsenal's No 1 himself, complete with a personal message.

Festive Funday

Four hundred young Arsenal fans flocked to Emirates Stadium on Thursday, January 3 for the Junior Gunners' Festive Funday. The eagerly-anticipated annual event saw the JGs enjoy an action-packed day in the company of the Gunners' first-team squad.

A day in the life

Throughout the year, Gunners stars invited Junior Gunners into their lives in the shape of the 'Day In The Life' feature on the JG website. Where else could you find out that Theo Walcott likes porridge for breakfast and that it takes him precisely 18 minutes to drive to training?!

SOCCER SCHOOLS

PLAY THE ARSENAL WAY™

Arsenal Soccer Schools ran courses throughout the United Kingdom. Girls and boys of all ability levels took part in the courses, learning to play the 'Arsenal Way'. Twelve football mad youngsters were specially selected by Arsenal Soccer Schools to form a guard of honour for the teams when Arsenal Ladies hosted Liverpool.

There are three levels of Junior Gunners membership, depending on your age:

Welcome to our world:
aged 0 to 3 years old.

WELCOME TO OUR WORLD

Team JG: 4 to 11 year olds.

TEAM JGs

Young Guns: 12 to 16 year olds.

Find out more and sign-up here:
alwaysaheadofthegame.com/junior

EMIRATES EXCELLENCE!

It's the home of the greatest team in the world. Enjoy these stunning photos of Emirates Stadium!

The season in photos!

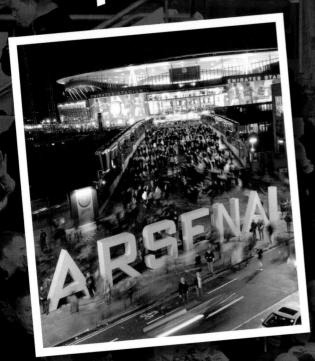

THE BIG ARSENAL QUIZ

Do you really know all there is to know about Arsenal? Are you a champion fan? This quiz will test you to the limits. Good luck!

1) Name the German star who signed for Arsenal in the summer of 2012.

2) What was the scoreline for the first two Premier League matches of the 2012/13 season?

3) True or false: the first league win of the campaign came at Old Trafford.

4) What nationality is Santi Cazorla?

5) Who did Arsenal beat 6-1 in September 2012?

6) What was the scoreline when Arsenal played Reading in October 2012?

7) Against which team did Mikel Arteta score two penalties in December 2012?

8) What was the scoreline when Arsenal played Bayern Munich in Germany during the 2012/13 UEFA Champions League?

9) Who scored the winning goal in the final league match of the 2012/13 season?

10) Arsenal finished the 2012/13 Premier League in what position?

11) In which year did Arsène Wenger become Arsenal manager?

12) And from which club did Wenger join the Gunners?

13) True or false: Steve Bould played as a centre-back for the Club.

14) Theo Walcott and Alex Oxlade-Chamberlain both joined from which south-coast side?

15) What nationality is Tomas Rosicky?

16) In what year was Arsenal FC founded: 1886 or 1906?

17) And in which year did Arsène Wenger win his first double for the Club?

18) Name the French striker who is Arsenal's top scorer.

19) Name the stadium the Club resided in before Emirates.

20) In which year did Arsenal go a whole league season unbeaten?

21) Name the German who kept goal for Arsenal during the 2005/06 UEFA Champions League campaign.

22) Who took the winning penalty in the shoot-out that won Arsenal the 2005 FA Cup?

23) What was the Club's first name?

24) Which Scot guided the Club to league titles in 1989 and 1991?

25) What nationality is Wojciech Szczesny?

26) From which team did Aaron Ramsey join the Gunners in 2008?

27) True or false: Mikel Arteta once played for Liverpool.

28) Name one of the two nations Carl Jenkinson has represented at youth level.

29) How many points did Arsenal amass during the 2012/13 league campaign?

30) And how many goals did they score?

Answers on Page 61

WORDSEARCH

Find the words in the grid. Words can go horizontally, vertically and diagonally in all eight directions.

G	K	B	H	P	I	H	S	N	O	I	P	M	A	H	C
W	K	K	C	C	X	B	C	F	C	U	P	C	K	J	S
H	D	K	T	G	N	N	Y	L	N	M	M	V	L	I	L
N	A	N	A	Y	E	L	L	O	V	H	J	L	L	A	B
N	U	O	M	C	S	K	W	L	T	H	R	V	R	D	M
X	Q	C	M	Y	R	W	X	W	D	R	E	Q	R	H	S
P	S	K	D	Y	E	R	X	K	E	R	O	A	T	C	T
R	L	O	G	Q	N	N	R	M	W	R	W	P	A	F	A
H	M	U	Q	Q	N	T	K	A	E	R	O	M	H	Y	D
N	A	T	G	T	U	N	R	L	O	U	P	C	T	Y	I
L	L	T	W	X	G	E	R	F	L	A	G	L	S	N	U
J	D	D	T	C	B	L	L	A	I	K	A	A	T	L	M
V	M	K	Y	R	M	R	O	G	D	N	M	K	E	G	T
J	X	X	T	M	I	G	N	M	E	T	V	Z	V	L	B
F	R	E	E	K	I	C	K	P	C	B	L	D	L	R	X
V	B	R	Z	M	K	X	K	T	D	L	N	R	C	M	F

BALL	FREEKICK	LEAGUE	SQUAD
CAMPAIGN	GOAL	MATCH	STADIUM
CHAMPIONSHIP	GUNNERS	PENALTY	TROPHY
CUP	HATTRICK	SCORE	VOLLEY
FORWARD	KNOCKOUT	SILVERWARE	

Answers on Page 61

GUESS WHO?

Can you guess who the four players are in the pictures below?

Answers on Page 61

CHARTING THE PROGRESS

Use this chart to refer back to to key moments in the 2012/13 season, and keep up-to-date with the equivalent moments in 2013/14 campaign. Enjoy!

Premier League	2012/13	2013/14
Final position	4th	
First home win	Southampton 6-1	
First away win	Liverpool 2-0	
First home draw	Sunderland 0-0	
First away draw	Stoke City 0-0	
First home defeat	Chelsea 2-1	
First away defeat	Norwich City 1-0	

Domestic Cup	2012/13	2013/14
FA Cup	Round 5: Blackburn Rovers	
League Cup	Round 5: Bradford City	

UEFA Champions League	2012/13	2013/14
Progress	Round 2: Bayern Munich	
First home win	Olympiacos 3-1	
First away win	Montpellier 2-1	
First home draw	None	
First away draw	Schalke 2-2	
First home defeat	Schalke 2-0	
First away defeat	Olympiacos 2-1	

Goals	2012/13	2013/14
First in Premier League	Podolski v Liverpool	
First in FA Cup	Podolski v Swansea City	
First in League Cup	Giroud v Coventry City	

QUIZ ANSWERS

Crossword, P42

```
            F
      P E N A L T Y
    B     R
T   A R S H A V I N         V
H   Y   R   H               I
R   E   R                   C
W E N G E R                 T
R   R   R               T   O
E   J U N I O R         A   R
W       N   O   M   H I G H B U R Y
J A C K   S   I   K     L   I
A       N   E M I R A T E S E
L       T   C   K     E     S
C           K
O   T H I E R R Y
T
```

Spot the Ball, P43

The Big Arsenal Quiz, P56

1)	Lukas Podolski	
2)	0-0	
3)	False, it was at Anfield	
4)	Spanish	
5)	Southampton	
6)	7-5 to Arsenal	
7)	West Bromwich Albion	
8)	2-0 to Arsenal	
9)	Laurent Koscielny	
10)	Fourth	
11)	1996	
12)	Grampus Eight Nagoya	
13)	True	
14)	Southampton FC	
15)	Czech	
16)	1886	
17)	1998	
18)	Thierry Henry	
19)	Arsenal Stadium	
20)	2004	
21)	Jens Lehmann	
22)	Patrick Vieira	
23)	Royal Arsenal	
24)	George Graham	
25)	Polish	
26)	Cardiff City	
27)	False, though he did play for Everton	
28)	Finland and England	
29)	73	
30)	72	

Wordsearch, P58

```
G K B H P I H S N O I P M A H C
W K K C C X B C F C U P C K J S
H D K T G N N Y L N M M V L I L
N A N A Y E L L O V H J L L A B
N U O M C S K W L T H R V R D M
X Q C M Y R W X W D R E Q R H S
P S K D Y E R X K E R O A T C T
R L O G Q N N R M W R W P A F A
H M U Q Q N T K A E R O M H Y D
N A T G T U N R L O U P C T Y I
L L T W X G E R F L A G L S N U
J D D T C B L L A I K A A T L M
V M K Y R M R O G D N M K E G T
J X X T M I G N M E T V Z V L B
F R E E K I C K P C B L D L R X
V B R Z M K X K T D L N R C M F
```

Guess Who, P59

1)	GIBBS	3)	CAZORLA
2)	WILSHERE	4)	GIROUD